NO
REFLECTION

From climbing the mountain of
childhood challenges, deceit, grief and
mental health struggles, to living your
best life

By Tina Wendy Roberts

DEDICATION

My dedication of this book is to my world,
right arm, best friend, my King and strong
Welsh man Harry.

Love you always, now and forever, your
Queen, Tina xxx

CONTENTS

ACKNOWLEDGMENTS

"Sometimes miracles are just good people with kind hearts."

I feel so lucky to have this feeling with family and so many special friends.

To my daughter, I'm a very proud mum of the woman you are today, an amazing mummy, wife and nurse. Harry was very proud to call you his daughter. Our grandsons were the greatest gift of all, and we thank you both for giving us the most wonderful grandchildren, the boys. We love them both to the moon and stars, all the world and back again.

My new home has a heart again. This place and my surroundings have given me love, companionship and happiness again that I thought was lost.

The hospital unit, TDC, I am forever grateful for their input and support.

All of this makes me the person I am today.

INTRODUCTION

My daughter's view of me at this low point in my life was that I was *dead behind the eyes*.

How would you feel if this was said to you? At the time I had no response. No feelings, no emotion, as if I didn't care. But of course I cared. I just didn't know how to show it, because I was numb and broken.

As Elton John sang...

"You could never know what it's like

Your blood, like winter, freezes just like ice,

And there's a cold, lonely light that shines from you

You'll wind up like the wreck you hide behind that mask you use."

My grandsons, they knew Nanna had been poorly and my interpretation to them during my recovery was "Nanna was a dummy in a shop window, trapped in a body that walked and talked". The boys found this funny, which was good as they weren't scared. I'm fine with this, as I would rather they be laughing than crying.

My first memory at the age of three years old is questionable. Was my dad chopping all the plugs off the appliances a healthy thing to witness? Should this be the earliest thing I can recollect?

Growing up thinking my mummy didn't love me, as I was always being pushed to my daddy. What did I do that was so wrong? Taken to see Dad's girlfriend and playing with her daughter, having beans on toast for tea. These are clear memories of a happy time which on reflection was also really wrong. Being asked to keep a secret and say I'd been to my granny's was a frequent occurrence.

Secrets and lies. This was introduced as a normal way of life for our family.

Finding myself as piggy in the middle with my parents, I was constantly pulled from pillar to post.

This caused emotional turmoil, which found me battling with who to choose.

Fast forward to my sister being married at 17 and leaving our home, leaving me as the only child in the household. I felt jealous she escaped, no more game playing for her.

At the age of 20 I was still seeing what I shouldn't. A grown woman being expected to lie to those closest to her. I realise now that all I had experienced to this point had caused me major trauma growing up.

My adult life, I see in three stages:

1. My first marriage gave me my daughter. I became a mother
2. My second marriage brought me to Wales
3. My third marriage gave me my pot of gold and happy ever after, Harry

Through this book I will acknowledge some potential trigger points which led to my reflection disappearing.

I want you to know that you can conquer anything that's thrown at you. Take it from me, I've been there, to my idea of hell and back anyway.

That journey for me and for you will be totally different, but one thing I've learned through this ordeal, is that hearing of other peoples' experiences can really help us get through things. That is what I want to do for you.

There is space at the back of the book for you to make any notes or have your own reflection time.

I will share the self-discovery on this difficult journey of ups and downs and tools that may help you personally, or your understanding of what your loved one may be going through right now. But I will also provide you with the light that shone and pulled me through the darkness. There was light at the end of the tunnel. This was something I was always told as a child, but it's only now that I see it.

THE BEGINNING

My mental health first started when I was a three-year-old little girl. I remember my mummy & daddy having an argument. The next thing my daddy was cutting all the plugs off everything. It must have been about an hour later; two plain clothed men came to the house and took my daddy away. He was gone for about two weeks.

As a child I thought this was something that I had done wrong. I was told he had gone away to work, and of course as a little one I didn't question this. But I wonder if I knew it was a lie.

Lots more things happened through the years.

Growing up as a child was never easy for my sister & I. With 14 months between us, close in age, we saw a lot. But for some reason, it always seemed to be me there. I don't recall my sister (who I dearly love) in the picture.

On the whole I was a happy child despite the fact that my mummy & daddy continued to argue.

One incident when I was about eight years old, my parents had a row. My mummy didn't want me to stay with her. I didn't know why this was and I still don't to this day.

My dad had no choice but to take me with him. I was taken to see his girlfriend at the time. I remember playing outside with her daughter and having beans on toast for tea. Being a child, this was an adventure, it was fun, I had a new friend. It certainly didn't bother me at that moment in time.

But then I knew this was wrong as it wasn't my mummy. More secrets and lies.

To be told by your parent "You have to say you went to Granny's" was a command that I followed. What else was I supposed to do? I didn't want to be the cause of any rows.

I was feeling confused. Why didn't my mummy want me? Was I such a difficult child?

I'm still confused now and wonder if this was Mum's way of coping. Perhaps she thought that by sending me off with him, he would be less likely to stray.

Sadly, me being in his company didn't stop him. Dad was a womaniser, and my mum didn't deserve this.

My sister and I were two children stuck in the middle. I would be left with our dad; she would go with our mum.

Our dad continued to have different affairs through their marriage. My sister got married at the age of 17 so she escaped the mayhem of the secrets and lies. In the end Mum had had enough of Dad's womanising ways. She left him. She had no choice but to leave I suppose, but I felt alone and unwanted again, even at the age of 20. I knew it was the right thing for Mum and accepted her decision. It was right for her and right for us, because it needed to stop. She finally said "Enough.".

Dad tried to win her back. He was saying the right things to Mum, as I don't think he ever thought she would leave him. Being together from the age of 14, first loves, married at 17 while expecting my sister and experiencing parenthood together. A caravan as their first home and my sister's cot being in a drawer is a story I recall being told by my mum. They had to grow up fast and deal with a lot at a young age.

Now with my mum gone, living with my dad was very difficult. As I felt I couldn't visit her without being questioned about what she was doing, who she was seeing and how she was coping without him. I felt my time with Mum was mine and should not be questioned. It was my private time with my mum which was special between us. It was nice to be mum & daughter again. He had blown it. But he was trying to get information to keep in my mum's good books. It turns out he was still keeping secrets.

The latest woman my dad was having an affair with was someone Mum and I both worked with. I was told of the affair by one of our work colleagues. More secrets to keep. How could I tell my mum? Even though she had left, it was not my story to tell. It would add more salt in the wound. This was not fair on anyone. And I was piggy in the middle again.

I was so upset I walked out of work and this time I confronted my dad.

I said "For the first time in your life, tell the truth. I can't cope with any more secrets and lies!"

He confirmed it. I felt so let down by my dad and devastated for my mum, she didn't deserve this. **Mum just did not deserve this.**

I felt forced to keep yet another secret, as the alternative of breaking my mum's heart was not something I wanted to do. It was too much for me to keep having to do this. Facing my mum knowing this secret, was so unfair. My dad was just so selfish, putting me in this situation. It was a burden on me.

It took all my mum's strength to give my dad his marching orders and I knew this.

I told my dad his actions were unforgivable. Putting extra pressure on me, his daughter who at only 20 years old is still playing piggy in the middle.

I wondered when it would be my life to live and be free of all the secrets and lies.

I didn't like the way this all made me feel inside. I knew it was wrong.

On reflection it's no wonder I was a bit rebellious as a child and going into my teen years. My actions never involved the police or anything, but I was just angry and defiant. Doing my thing, as teenagers do. Not only was I trying to cope with hormones but also what was going on with my parents was always on my mind, and I was growing up thinking my mum didn't love me. But she did, I just didn't know this until years later.

Mum always regretted her decision of pushing me to my dad. One day she asked me if I knew she loved me. My reply was "No, as you always pushed me to my dad." Mum was so sorry about this. But I didn't hold it against her.

Going back to the last secret I was bearing… Mum came to see me one day and jokingly said "I wonder if it's J*** G********?" I just stared at her in disbelief, my eyes grew wider and I felt relieved. I nodded my head and felt the release of this burden from my shoulders. I cried and with tears running down my face I said "Sorry".

I was so sorry that I couldn't tell her sooner, but she knew the reason why. After all this time I felt numb but glad it was finally over. No more secrets and lies.

TINA'S TOOLS:

Be kind & true to yourself & show yourself love

"Letting some people go is good for soul, great for your mind, and magnificent for your life."

THE THICK FOG

Life was moving on for me. I was engaged to be married to my first husband. My wedding was all booked, exciting times ahead. I would finally be able to live a normal life with no secrets and lies. At the age of 20 this was a big relief, and I was full of hope. Knowing I can truly be my own person and not having to carry the burden of past history.

Two years on I discovered we were having our first baby. I always wanted to be a mum and always dreamed of having a daughter. Excited and scared all at the same time as most expectant mums-to-be feel, I assume.

One thing I knew was that I did not want for my child to be brought up with secrets and lies. This is not what to teach your child, I had learned from this. I had experienced it and I knew that it affected me.

My daughter was born by emergency C-section weighing 6lbs 10oz, simply perfect. Life was good with my new baby.

The news of our new arrival was shared with our families. Messages of congratulations poured in with cards and gifts for her.

My mum at last was moving on with life. Fortunate to meet Cyril who became my stepdad, it was nice to see her happy at last. Cyril was a good man, he looked after Mum well.

One day I recall my mother-in-law coming to see me. I knew something was wrong. I remember the feeling of dread, like a flashback to my childhood years. I was going to find out something I didn't want to hear. I felt like I knew what it was like to be in my mum's shoes for the first time.

I went looking for one thing and found another. A letter from another woman and complete devastation set in. My husband was having an affair with his brother's wife, our daughter's Auntie. He didn't deny it. Our family broke down. I was so certain that I didn't want a life like my mum had experienced for me and my daughter. I was heartbroken but the trust was gone, and our marriage was over.

All of this happening was quite raw for Mum. And strangely enough my dad gave some support, was this guilt on his part perhaps? Who knows?

Mum married Cyril. The age difference of 11 years didn't matter at first. But became more apparent as the years went by, with Mum getting old before her time. She was always so young at heart, very sociable and enjoyed life before.

Cyril passed away at the age of 80. Mum's world was completely upside down. Living with my sister straight away, she eventually moved into her own bungalow being alone for the first time. She hadn't had much contact with friends for a while. It was tough for her and I'm sure she felt abandoned and lonely, as he was her life.

Mum's life began to pick up when she saw the family she still had around her and the love that was there. I understand now how significant this is. Having holidays in Wales she got to spend time with us and her grandchildren more, and the smile came back to her face.

My life moved on as well. A night out with a friend introduced me to my future husband, but I didn't know this at the time. I am grateful to him, for he brought my daughter and I to Wales.

I loved Wales. A new life, a new start for us all.

I still remember my daughter's first morning of school. Feeling nerves and excitement for her, she settled in well, bless her. Our first morning of school involved a bus journey, it was an adventure. She soon made friends, chatting to a lady called Yvonne while we waited for the bus, with her little girl Emma. To this day I'm still grateful for their friendship.

We all settled in very well to our new life in Wales. Life was good. In time I found myself a job as a catering assistant at Holywell community hospital. The additional responsibility of being the acting-up cook when the main cook was off, gave me a great sense of pride. I loved this job; it suited all of our lives.

In time, our daughter was at the age of going to high school. She grasped the challenge with both hands. The years were flying by happily in Wales. I'm thankful for this.

However, my happiness was short-lived as I fell poorly and had to have a hysterectomy. Many women struggle with the loss of their womb, but for me, I had struggled with periods since the age of 13. Following my emergency caesarean, which was lifesaving for both me and my daughter, I'd suffered with pain from scar tissue and trauma of the operation. So the procedure was a no-brainer for me. The operation went well, and I was soon back at home recovering. I felt free, at last, from pain and discomfort in this area of my body. I've heard that women hold stress and trauma in their pelvic area, I wonder if this had impacted me?

With the support of my daughter and husband my life soon returned to normal and I was back working within four months.

Feeling happy with my recovery and job, life resumed. But I was feeling the strain of balancing things. I went without meals to pay for her love of dancing, as her dad was spending more money on drink than we had to spend on food.

Then the major blow. I was shocked to find out history was repeating itself. I found out that my husband was cheating on me.

"Is it me?" I ask myself. My first husband cheated with his brother's wife. Now here we are, my daughter is 13 years old and aware of what is going on this time around. This felt so unfair for us both, just when we were enjoying life, happy and settled.

I begin to think "Is it my fault?". It's like being the little girl again, secrets and lies are featuring in our lives.

It was a struggle for us both, we were feeling let down. I didn't want this for my daughter, but he was her dad, he had brought her up.

We stayed living under the same roof for some time. Somehow we managed it. We were able to settle back into our lives, but our marriage was over. The trust was broken. For months we lived amicably but the time came where we had to draw a line.

At this point I just felt completely shattered. I didn't even want to leave the house. Getting dressed seemed like a massive task, but I did it.

How was I going to cope? My daughter, she was my reason for moving on, but life was a constant worry. The biggest mistake I made was trying to be Mum and Dad. And I realise now we can only really be one person, and Mum was all I needed to be.

I was consumed with guilt that it was just the two of us again.

This guilt can cause you to over-compensate, but you can truly only be one person, don't you think? I know that many parents do try to take on both roles, as many of my friends have done the same. The additional pressure that is felt in this situation is a lot for people to deal with. The lack of support can cause you to feel overwhelmed and it's difficult to cope.

We somehow managed to get on with our lives. I carried on with my job at the hospital and I still remember the moment I was asked to go out with them all. I felt nervous about going out again, but it was time for me to get on with my life. This is where our lives were about to change, but I wasn't aware how.

The night out was a barbeque in The Rock in Lloc. I smile every time I say that out loud. Not just because it rhymes but because it's where I met Harry. He was truly like a breath of fresh air. I was feeling down on the floor and he made me laugh.

The taxi didn't turn up that night, so we all walked home. The long windy road with trees on either side was something that had been described to me by a fortune teller. "You will meet the love of your life," she said. She wasn't wrong. I didn't realise at the time that he would become *my pot of gold.*

We had our first date a few days later. It was lovely to feel special again after all this time, but also scary. Wondering if I can trust someone else, after being cheated on twice already. We went on quite a few dates. It was lovely to be treated like a queen and made to feel special.

Harry told me he loved me after three weeks. Wow I wasn't sure I wanted to hear this. "Is this too soon?" I was thinking. It was scary but also lovely all at the same time. Embracing all these new feelings was like a whirlwind, and there was not just me to consider. Questions like "Can I do this again? Will it all go wrong?". I needed to be strong and chose to make a big decision and surrender to the possibility that this could all go right.

Our lives moved on very quickly. Harry was introduced to my daughter. Life was good. After two years we bought our first house together.

Feeling happy and supported, with no more worry of trying to give all to my daughter alone. We married six years later and it was wonderful. It was so nice to feel safe and loved. Also, Harry got a daughter who he adored and would've bought her the world and more if he could. It was lovely to see Stepdad and daughter together. It was special to be part of, a family at last. And I truly got my pot of gold.

Even though life was good, after downsizing our family home to a bungalow, everything caught up with me. I experienced my first breakdown and admission to the Ablett unit. However, I came through this quickly with support from my family.

My mum continued to have holidays with us. Wales was her second home. When Mum's car went bang, Harry and I managed to find my mum a replacement here in Wales. With my sister and brother-in-law, we all chipped in and bought the car for our mum. This gave her independence back and took the pressure off those she had been reliant upon for their taxi services. Life was good for us all. As a family unit, we continued to have lovely holidays in Wales, all four generations included. It was precious watching Mum with her great grandsons who she adored.

One Thursday evening 21st December 2018, Harry became unwell. Up three times in the night, it was so unlike him. He was in tears, which many men don't like to show. I knew this was serious, so I phoned for an ambulance. Rapid response arrived. They weren't happy with how Harry presented and said he needed to go to hospital. A shortage of ambulances resulted in me taking my husband in. Arriving at 8:30am we were in for a long day. But being sat in a chair for all this time was not comfortable for Harry. I refused to let him stay in this situation in pain. He needed to rest and couldn't as he was. So I took him home to sleep in a bed.

Helping him to get ready the next morning, we were both exhausted and anxious. We did not know what was about to be revealed or how the day would unfold. Arriving back at the hospital we waited patiently for his scan.

I remember it so clearly. At 11:30am he was taken from me for the scan. 11:45am I watched the Doctor on the computer. Ten minutes later I asked "Is that my husband's results?" and his answer was "Yes.". I just knew this wasn't good.

Our lives were devastated by the results we were given. Harry was diagnosed with pancreatic cancer. It was 22nd December, just three days before Christmas. This was such a hard thing to process and far too much to bear.

We left the hospital with no words, just silence. How do we tell our daughter and son-in-law and the boys the terrible news?

How I drove home I don't know. We first went to our daughter's home to break the awful news. I knew I needed to find the strength to do this and tell her something so horrible. We told all our nearest and dearest. How we got through Christmas I will never know, but we did it as a family.

Our daughter suggested I book a weekend away while Harry was still well enough to enjoy it, before his treatment would start. I booked Lake Vyrnwy. I'm so glad we had this time together. Precious memories were made. We had four seasons with sunshine, wind, rain and lots of snow. This was breath-taking.

Home and back to reality. Harry's battle for life began. He was so brave.

Harry went on to have treatment which firstly consisted of a picc-line being fitted for his chemotherapy. He was my brave gentle giant. Never complained and took everything in his stride. Such a courageous and unique man.

Harry endured nine weeks of the cancer and bravely fought. Being asked by your loved one "Am I going to die?" was devastating. How do you answer this? I said "You're going no-where and we are going to live the best life we can. Let's focus on this, because you're going nowhere."

We managed to carry on somehow and enjoy the good things in life. Our precious family, grandchildren, friends and much much more. He battled with all his might and held on as long as he could, but sadly our gentle Welsh giant Harry, my husband, stepdad, loving taidy closed his eyes for the last time and fell asleep on the 22nd February 2019.

How will I cope without my right arm, best friend and soulmate? My everything and more.

After the shock of Harry's passing, I felt I had to wake up the next day and put a big smile on my face as it was my 60th birthday. He told me he wanted me to have this special day and to enjoy it with the boys and family. It was a big challenge to carry out Harry's wishes. Words were not needed between us, we were so close, we knew each other inside out. He always used to say "Your face says it all."

The morning of my 60th birthday arrived. It felt like I was in a nightmare. But reality was that Harry had gone. All I could think was "How do I live without my everything, without my pot of gold?".

I somehow found my strength and got myself ready to go and celebrate my 60th birthday. Driving down to my daughter's, it was the first time I'd seen my grandsons. The eldest ran and clung to me burying his head, "Please don't cry, Nanna's OK?". There was a lovely big chocolate cake with candles, they both sang their little hearts out in English and then in Welsh for Taidy. It was truly lovely. How I held it together I'll never know. After that we all got ready to go out for a birthday meal.

Somehow, we pulled it off and celebrated my birthday. That's what Harry wanted. He did his best to be with us, but it was not to be. I think he wanted me to have this special day for me and the boys with friends and family.

We had lots of things to sort out to arrange Harry's funeral. The weeks flew by. We did everything Harry wanted, bless him. With a tribute for my brave lion heart who was still putting me first. The funeral was a brilliant send-off and testament to how well-loved Harry was. His tarmac colleagues and workmen gave him a standing ovation as we entered the crematorium. As hard as it was, we all said goodbye to our gentle Welsh giant.

Thank you darling for loving me. 22 glorious years of pure love, memories to treasure and in my heart forever.

Eventually we all settled down into a routine and life resumed as normal as it could be. It was impossible to be 'normal' as it was a new situation, a new way of life. I somehow managed to get on with the day-to-day and to give myself the time I needed to sort through things.

I decided to go back to work a few months later. This was the hardest thing for me to do. Everyone was so lovely. The first week went quickly with the support of colleagues. I still missed Harry with all of my heart. But at this time work was what I needed to try to help me adapt to walking my new path.

A few months later we all went on a family holiday. My daughter, son-in-law, grandsons, mother-in-law and me. This was just what the doctor ordered. It seemed so strange to do this without Harry. But I told myself "This is my life now. I am walking a new path and trying to live the best life I can without my world, my everything and more.". The holiday was enjoyed by all.

I returned back to work, but in time work just got too much for me. I felt I couldn't cope. I couldn't give everything to the patients anymore. This was the beginning of being unwell, but I didn't realise it. The doctor signed me off work for a short time. I returned, thinking I was ready, but in hindsight it was too soon.

My diary had some lovely distractions to look forward to. A Caribbean cruise. Plus, I was also doing a 10km run in Colwyn Bay on October 26th. This was a challenge in itself. These events are organised by my personal trainer and his colleague. The training was good, and I felt on top of the world for a short time. And I did it! I managed to complete the 10K, what a great feeling! I had tears of joy.

The cruise was just around the corner. The travel industry was being hit by companies going bust, and that happened to our airline. Luckily for us as it was an all-inclusive holiday P&O were honouring the trips. Phew! But anxiety began to kick in. I had realised this was the same ship Harry and I had spent time on previously only 13 months ago. I was feeling so nervous and anxious, not knowing how I would feel.

This was a worrying time for so many reasons. Everything was escalating, everything seemed a bigger deal as I wasn't feeling my best. Then confirmation came through that we had our flights again and all was good. Now ready for holiday, my dog Prince went to the kennels. A luxury one for him.

We are now on our way. Feeling excited, anxious and nervous all at the same time

Everything went well at the airport. I had realised I had worried for nothing. We arrived in the Caribbean. Waiting to board the ship a photo is taken for ID. Arriving on board I had mixed emotions. This is the same cruise ship Harry and I were on. I thought

"Have I done the right thing in doing the cruise?" I can see Harry everywhere.

With the internet not being its best and a long way from home I felt anxious and isolated. The first evening meal was lovely, as was the ship. But the Caribbean itself was not what I had visualised. Where were the idyllic beaches I had been sold? How about the perfectly positioned relaxing spaces we see advertised? Home sickness set in.

Approaching our second week I began to feel unsettled. "Oh dear this is not good" I thought. I was trying to stay positive, but the warning signs were here, something was up. I carried on as best as I could. But when my friend announced she was having a day out by herself, I panicked. I got through the day alone and luckily enjoyed the most beautiful evening for a sunset cruise. That final night was the highlight of the holiday for me. It was stunning but I also knew I'd be going home tomorrow.

As soon as I saw my family I broke down in floods of tears. I felt heart broken. I felt unwell. The cruise was definitely not the right thing for me to have done. I received the biggest bear hug from my son-in-law, this is what I miss the most from Harry. Someone's protective arms around me.

My daughter called the doctors, and I was given anti-depressants. I didn't want to feel like this anymore. I was hoping the tablets would help me as I knew I was unwell. I didn't want to admit this to myself or anyone else. I didn't want to feel like a failure again.

Grief is an awful thing. It comes in waves. It just takes over and you have no control. I was taking the medication and functioning the best I could, but I wasn't feeling any better.

I was back at work, but I wasn't coping. I was overwhelmed. I wasn't eating or sleeping properly. Others could see I was unwell. One day I just walked out and felt like I had to run away. "Get me out!" was in my head. I drove straight to my GP and I was signed off immediately. I was in crisis mode.

Looking back, I am so glad I had the self-awareness to walk out of the building when I did, as this protected not only myself but those around me from seeing me have a melt-down.

I was assigned a CPN (Community Psychiatric Nurse) and a Health Care Support Worker. I was admitted to the Ablett unit again. My second admission, yet equally as scary as the first, seven years earlier. I continued to withdraw both physically and mentally. Unable to do basic care for myself, trapped in a body that didn't work. "Dead behind the eyes."

TINA'S TOOLS:

Get dressed even when you don't feel like it

"And today if all you did was hold yourself together, I am proud of you."

THE MOUNTAIN TO CLIMB

Here I am again on the second admission to hospital feeling alone and scared. I really didn't want to admit I was in crisis again. It felt like a prison, only one where I was allowed to walk around freely. But sometimes the doors were on lock-down so this wasn't possible to do then.

Feeling a failure again being back in hospital. My cruise should have helped me to feel fab. But it did the complete opposite. It made me realise how much I missed Harry. The saddest thing of all was when my daughter asked me why her family weren't enough for me. She was in floods of tears and so was I. Because at this point, I was so ill I had to admit this to myself and my family, I didn't feel they were enough. This broke my heart. But the grief and the loss of Harry was just too much to bear. I couldn't hide how I felt as my daughter asked me to be truthful. I can still see her face now. I would hate to see her ever feeling as I did.

Hospital I found very tough on this admission. During my five weeks there, I was told the worst news. My mum was very poorly, and the outlook wasn't good. It was getting near to Christmas. My daughter made sure I was able to have Christmas with the family. They picked me up Christmas day so we could all be together. It was lovely, I hated saying goodbye. But I was able to see them on boxing day as well.

Mum was growing increasingly poorly and this time it was my daughter's turn to break devastating news. My mum was dying. This hit me so hard. Thankfully I was able to leave the hospital and go to Leicester so I could say my goodbyes to my mum.

How was I going to do this? We arrived in Leicester. Going inside to see my mum was very tough. I was so shocked that she looked so tiny in her hospital bed. I thanked Mum for being my mum & told her I loved her. The time came to leave. I didn't want to go. All my mum asked of me was to get well. I felt so guilty that I was unable to help care for her. It broke my heart in two to say goodbye, knowing this was the last time I would see her alive.

I'm so thankful I got the chance to say goodbye. She didn't want me to cry. The fact she was still thinking of me was everything. It just didn't seem real that my mum was dying. It felt like another bad dream.

I couldn't bear the thought of losing someone else. I just felt like life wasn't worth living. Despite this after the funeral I was discharged from the Ablett unit.

Once back home at the bungalow I had never felt so alone. I just wanted to run away and hide. I couldn't cope with how I felt. My world was even more destroyed. "What's the point?" I thought.

This is when I thought I would regain control. Although it was detrimental to my health. I stopped my medication. I just wanted to take control back, but without realising I was becoming even more ill with the action I had taken.

All I wanted was Harry, but I was feeling more guilt for feeling this way and upsetting those close to me. I had to admit to myself that I was more poorly than ever and went to the clinic. They said they had no choice but to give me the depo injection. I feared I would be allergic as so many medications don't agree with me. But nobody listened, the decision was taken away from me.

I may have mental health, but I do know my own body. Just because we are 'in crisis' we should be listened to and respected, as we are human and have lived our lives to this moment in time. The depo injection was given in spite of my protest. Within two hours I was reacting badly. My body didn't like it, and neither did I. By the end of the week I was worse. I was dragging my leg. I had a blank expression. I just wasn't myself.

My health care support worker came to see me. We went out for a walk. She was concerned for my wellbeing. Immediately she contacted my CPN to say how I was presenting myself. I felt so anxious. "What's happening to me?" I was thinking. No control, feeling scared and vulnerable, my anxiety levels were through the roof. I knew where all this was heading, a third admission to the Ablett unit.

Feeling scared I didn't want to go. But my fears were confirmed. I was being admitted to hospital again. I felt let down, and once again it was medicine being forced on me. Just like the first time, when I'd tried to refuse diazepam because it made me feel drunk and unsafe on my feet. They saw this as refusal and being defiant and insisted. However, when my daughter raised her concerns and said the same, they agreed to omit it from my medications. Her words to them were "My mum is ill and not stupid; she does have a mind and should be listened to." Yet here we were again. This wouldn't have happened. I had said I would be allergic to the depo and I was right, they just assumed it was my mental health talking.

PLEASE LISTEN AS WE KNOW OUR BODIES.

I presented with Parkinson's symptoms. I had the blank expression, the dragging of the leg and jerking movements. The doctors need to listen.

PEOPLE NEED TO LISTEN. PATIENTS DO HAVE A MIND!

While in the Ablett I became very unwell. I had cellulitis in my leg and was admitted to A&E. My experience here wasn't a good one. While I was waiting in a cubicle to be seen I was on the edge of the room looking out, a nurse whom I knew spoke to me like a piece of rubbish, someone I had worked with. I had mental health, I was and am a human being. She shouted "Get in there" as if I were a dog. How can you ever forget this type of treatment and how does it possibly help you to get better? Soon I was moved on to a ward with IV antibiotics. Everyone else was kind and pleased to help and support me. This is what we need.

Do I complain about the way in which I was treated by that particular individual? I still wonder this. Does holding on to the feeling damage me further? I'm sure she will have forgotten. But what concerns me is that she could be doing it to other vulnerable people every single day. And that is not right.

It was lovely to see my daughter after all this time. I was in the main hospital for a few days. With my leg now on the mend, back to the Ablett I go. Despite it getting better I was still in extreme pain. I was feeling more and more depressed. My leg all swollen, mobility impacted, all my family were concerned. I just want to get well.

It had become my task to start to climb that mountain, I needed to get well and go home. Dr Roberts felt I'd be ready for home in a week. But with no hot water I told them "I can't go home". It proves how ill I was as I had been showering in cold water, even washed my hair like this. That is not my preference at all. My son-in-law discovered my boiler needed a part. I'm so grateful for having people around me who can help me figure things out. Very often we take it for granted that we should know how to fix things – like a broken boiler, but when you are a person of older age, alone, how do we know who to call? Luckily the part was ordered, it was fixed, and I could go home at last. My daughter did my shopping and stocked my cupboards so I had food.

Despite the house being ready, I arrived home to the bungalow feeling scared. "I don't want to live here anymore" I thought. I can't do it, too many memories. Harry and I were the heart of the bungalow, the heart was broken, he wasn't here. He had gone.

Finally admitting to myself I needed somewhere else to live, I was struggling big time. I felt so lonely, so vulnerable. Arriving at my friend's doorstep in flood of tears, I admit I can't cope and don't want to be there, in the bungalow anymore. She rang my sister and told her I was in bits. My friend said "You need to be with your sister, she needs her family support as well. H***** and I can't do it all and covid hasn't helped."

At this point I'd ran out of my tablets and needed another prescription. My sister and brother-in-law arrived on the Monday morning to take me home with them for a holiday. This kind of love and support is invaluable, to just feel safe and secure is what we all need. A doctor's appointment was made, and my medication all sorted. Now off to Leicester for a break.

I always remember Mum telling me she went to a fortune teller who told her that she had two daughters, one would be fine in life and the other would struggle, have traumas and travel, but would be OK in the end. I know which one is me. And I'm so grateful to my sister for being the strong one, and for holding me in a safe space when I needed her.

TINA'S TOOLS:

Take deep breaths & count to ten

"Let the clouds remind you that if your heart is feeling heavy you are allowed to cry."

Tina Wendy Roberts

SEEING CLEARLY

My Auntie Shelagh always said "Tina there is always light at the end of the tunnel. When one door closes another one opens." I believe she is right with this statement.

Arriving in Leicester for a 'holiday' this is the start of seeing clearly. A break away from my new normal so that I could process things without the distraction of the feelings that I felt while I was in the bungalow.

It gave me time to reflect and to make some decisions. I know I can't continue to live there. I won't survive here but feeling scared and afraid. "What do I do and where can I live?"

This unsettled feeling sent my mind into overdrive, feeling anxious and wobbly. "Where will my future be?"

I settled in at my sisters and unpacked everything. We sat down to dinner a few hours later. I remember it being very nice after the long day. I felt content going off to bed. Tomorrow is another day.

I did not know that what happened on this new day would be the start of something so simple yet so positive. Up and showered I went out for a walk with Ellie, the dog, around the park. At first this seems too big for me to do but putting the best foot forward I did this. And it continued. Every day was a walk around the park with Ellie. I was expected to do this every day and at times I really didn't want to. But I was doing it to please everyone and conform to their expectations. I've always put others before myself or perhaps the label is that I've been a 'people pleaser'. But I know I need to start putting myself first, and this walking is positive steps in the right direction. "My aim is to get well and everyone else wants that for me too." I had to tell myself.

The first week was going fast. My CPN was doing a team call. She was not happy with me as she discovered I'd not been taking my thyroxine properly nor my tablets. I don't know why I stopped; I just can't tell you. I felt disappointed with myself that I allowed myself to do this. I think really, it's because my medication felt like it controlled me, rightly or wrongly I had to be in control of me. Being unable to find the words and explain my fears maybe this medication was a muse or distraction. But then I finally admitted to my sister and my CPN that "I don't want to live in the bungalow anymore." A weight lifted off my shoulders. I spoke out and shared my feelings. But where do I go from here?

My CPN mentioned an independent living set-up. It piqued my interest. I had nothing to lose. So, I agreed to her writing a letter on my behalf, sharing all the details about my mental health journey. This was a stage of acceptance. I felt ok with this but very nervous. I had spent a lovely two weeks with my sister, spending time with family. I came so far during this short time. I am so grateful. My son-in-law drove down to pick me up. We had a nice lunch in the pub before we headed home.

After a lovely few weeks away, reality was setting back in on return to the bungalow. The anxiety, fear and loneliness are not a nice feeling, and I was worried I would feel them before I even stepped foot through the door. We arrived home safe. I put my shopping away. My son-in-law stayed for a while, then of course had to go home to the family

Feeling alone again and scared. I just didn't want to be alone. It was not a nice feeling. My CPN had sent the letter on my behalf to Awel Y Dyffryn, putting me forward to be considered to move to independent living. It was a waiting game.

As we were still in times of the global pandemic, I was introduced to new technology. An interview on the Teams page on the computer with the manager was a success. First step done and an application form was sent out to me.

It was Christmas time again. I was invited to stay with my daughter and her family, which was exactly what I needed.

I'd taken the form with me and she helped me fill it all in. She is so much better at putting it down in the right way. I'm not very good in getting things across correctly sometimes, at articulating myself. Also the process is a bit daunting.

Feeling excited and slightly nervous, I knew I'd made the right decision in deciding to move. But I felt scared and frightened and guilty all at the same time. Thinking I'd let Harry down by not staying in our home, in the bungalow.

I had to think about this long and hard. I knew being there was no good for my recovery, for my mental health. I soon came to realise that Harry will be forever in my heart and would always be with me no matter where I was.

Fast forward to the New Year and I received the letter I had been waiting for. A letter to go and view the flats. My anxiety levels were high again, or perhaps it was excited nerves. I've been told so many times that anxiety or nerves and excitement are the same feeling, but they are perceived differently. I wish I could've seen it as excitement back then. My mind was whirling like a spinning top again, I was so wobbly, but I took deep breaths and powered on as I knew this was the way forward.

It was January 27th. My daughter came with me to view the flat. Once inside I had a good feeling. Pleasantly surprised by the size, so much bigger than I expected. Silence fell over me. Panic inside feeling "Now I know this is it, this is real". But I went home feeling positive. I was making this change for me, for myself, to help me feel better and get better.

It was a while before I was offered the apartment in writing, but I held it in my hands, this was real. I had until the February 2nd to make my decision. To choose whether I was going to take the flat or stay in our bungalow. Undecided, scared, guilty for wanting to move, but for my mental health I knew I had to put myself first. This wasn't something I was used to doing so was not an easy thing to do. It was new territory. I was used to having decisions made **for** me. So, taking such a big step, when you've never done this before is scary.

It was time to get well and focus on the future. I'd made a promise to my mum I would get well and having my daughter and her family, her boys, I realised I had everything to live for.

TINA'S TOOLS:

Know your triggers

"Be strong enough to stand alone, smart enough to know when you need help, and brave enough to ask for it."

Tina Wendy Roberts

LIVING YOUR BEST LIFE

"Make the rest of your life the best of your life."

Well, here's to living my best life, to grasping life with both hands and being totally grateful for the lessons life has taught me. After climbing that bloody big mountain including four years of ups and many downs, including two Ablett admissions of five and nine weeks respectively, it's not been easy.

I realise that without the wonderful support of my daughter, family and extended family, also very special friends (you know who you are) during the biggest battle of our lives supporting Harry in his nine weeks battling for life, it would have been even more unbearable. Our beautiful grandsons, the boys, and fur baby TJ who were Taidy Harry's world, they kept us hopeful. These young innocent lives need to be protected and nurtured so they don't experience the things those before them have lived (me and their mum). The eldest grandson drew a picture of all of us for Taidy Harry. I've framed it and it takes pride of place on the bedroom wall.

Without all this support I dread to think how my life would be now.

Family is so important. But at the same time sometimes things can feel too close, as they all are grieving too. Together we learn to cope as a unit, if everyone communicates and can explain how they are feeling. For a time I couldn't find the words, and that impacted on us all.

From the dark times and depths, you can hit rock bottom. But from here it is possible to gain strength - from somewhere. Having faith and belief that the main man in my life is always here with me comforts me. Harry is guiding me now. I felt so scared when he left this Earth, that I had lost him. But now I see signs, and I take comfort in these.

As Marvin Gaye said in the song 'Ain't No Mountain High Enough'...

"My love is alive, way down in my heart,

Although we are miles apart"

Through this new stage of life, I know that he is happy and at peace. I can hear Harry saying

"THANK F**K for that, I can have peace of mind too". We are both in a place of peace.

My journey continues to grow and with it my confidence does too. I'm back doing all the things I love. I owe big thanks to my support worker who turned up one Monday morning and said, "You're going to the Hwb today" and I can honestly say I never looked back.

I am part of a choir. I attend art class. It's been excellent for my mental health as you lose yourself for a few hours, spending time mindfully just doing that thing you are doing.

Outside of the new accommodation things are moving quickly. The bungalow needed to be let out, to help cover my own rent. I was feeling anxious about getting the right tenants and all the responsibility of doing things the right way. But I did it. Lots of furniture was sold as there was too much for the flat. Everything was getting sorted and falling into place.

I signed the paperwork and official moving date April 15th. This was a massive step. Panic mode again. But "I am ready for this; I am doing the right thing" I kept reaffirming to myself. I had lots of questions, lots of "what ifs…". But instead of the outcome being negative I had to think of the positives. I was saying "Yes" for what felt like the first time in my life.

I was taking control. It's the best decision for me.

The Manager of our accommodation tells me now, that when I first moved in, I wasn't even able to smile, if I wanted to. I didn't realise how poorly I still was at this time. But looking back now I can see how far I've come.

I took comfort in taking lots of things to the charity shop as well knowing it would help a lot of people. Plus, there is something really satisfying and therapeutic in having a clear out and getting organised. But clearing the bungalow was not easy. Emotionally it was so difficult. Physically it was tiring. Practically there was a lot to do, like skip orders.

Then the date, it was not a good weekend for it was Harry's 3rd anniversary and my birthday. My heart just wasn't in it. I appreciated the organising of things by my daughter and her family, all their time, but "not this weekend". I didn't want to face it. But it all had to be done.

I felt as if I was intruding on Harry's life & personal things. I was so emotional going through all his lifelong treasures, his cob radio etc. But I had to think practically, sadly it was of no use to anyone. Harry's life in a skip, it felt wrong. But I can hear him now saying "Tina we are born with nothing & we leave this world with nothing, it's OK". With his strength still guiding me I was able to do this.

All the garage nearly emptied, the charity shops up town benefited with work stuff and a good day's work completed. My son-in-law, daughter and the boys did a good job. My birthday was the next day. It was made special with my daughter cooking dinner and the boys helping their daddy sort the garden. All of these distractions were just what I needed.

The night before the move my emotions were everywhere. My anxiety through the roof. I managed to stay calm, focusing on my breathing and did sleep quite well thankfully.

I remember it well, the morning is here, it's moving day. I was so nervous that everything was happening. The van arrived and it was getting loaded very fast. A friend came round to help, as well as my family. I was so grateful for the support.

Off we go up to the new flat, the smell of the carpets lovely and fresh. It was chaos but we started to organise things. My bed was the next thing to turn up, this makes a house a home. It was quickly put together and I knew that evening I would be spending my first night in my new bedroom. The day moved very fast. Lots was sorted.

It was eventually time for my first shower in my new abode, it all felt so personal. I was really ready for bed, absolutely exhausted but proud of how lovely it all looked. It wouldn't have happened without all my helpers on the day. My daughter for her organisation skills. Also, my son-in-law for the physical and practical handy man tasks.

That night on my own for the first time, I was feeling anxious, but I managed an odd hour's sleep. Back to the bungalow the next morning to sort through everything that had been stored in the attic for years. Although it was helpful, they had brought it down into the house, when I saw it, I just burst into tears. For me it looked like all of our life was now rubbish on the floor. I sobbed, it broke my heart, but it wasn't anyone's fault, it was just how I felt in that moment. Grief hits you unexpectedly.

I managed to pull myself together and we all got lots of sorting done. My close friends were there to help as well. I'm so grateful for their friendship and support always.

Life was settling down in my new abode. I just had the bungalow to finish getting sorted. With the help of special friends we got it done. I couldn't face going back, seeing it bare. So I decided to get a cleaning company in. For me this was self-preservation, I had to protect myself. I was vulnerable and this would have broken me. I would have gone backwards in my recovery. The bungalow was gleaming and ready for a new family to enjoy and put the heart back in to the home.

Now to start living my next life... the best I can, as this is all Harry wanted for me - to be happy.

The bungalow gained its new family fast. Some of these landlord duties weren't what I wanted to be dealing with, but I had to. I was so grateful to the Agent for sorting all the rest of the legal and complicated requirements that come with renting out your property.

My life started moving forwards slowly. One step at a time I introduced new activities that would help me more than I would even know.

Fitness and having a personal trainer made me accountable. I started to feel good knowing I was being more active. *"Nothing happens until something moves."* - Albert Einstein

Art lets me lose myself. *"Art is the journey of a free soul."* – Alev Ogus

Choir makes my heart sing. *"Sometimes music is the only medicine the heart and soul need."* - Unknown

The monthly forget-me-knot project is specifically aimed to bring people together, removing the feeling of isolation and loneliness.

Being part of a community helps me know I am supported beyond just my family and close friends.

Doing all of these things has helped my mental health immensely. So much so that my CPN started talking about discharging me for good. This was an amazing feeling, building my confidence knowing that others were seeing the improvements in me, as well as how I was feeling inside.

Going away on holiday abroad with a friend, my first experience without the family, since my recovery was like the icing on the cake. I felt free and alive.

"Once you learn how to create your own happiness no one can take it from you."

I was excited but nervous for a planned visit to Leicester to see the family. The first time in four years. The hotel was booked, and my friend and I were looking forward to introducing my past life to my friend. Sadly, she was poorly. I was thrown off-course and had a panic. But I soon realised that going alone was the best thing that could've happened. It gave me my independence back and I realised how capable I was of doing what I set out to.

"She believed she could, so she did." - R.S Grey

I went by myself, a tick off the bucket list. With a lot more things to come.

<u>TINA'S TOOLS</u>:

Take medication & consider alternative therapies

"Don't fight life when life wants to love you. Stop fighting and start loving your life for what it is and it's beautiful if you look deeply enough."

CONCLUSION

I am truly living my best life and loving it.

I never ever thought I would feel happiness again after losing my pot of gold. Even my photos smile back at me now, it's magical. It's been such a hard mountain to climb and I've finally reached the summit, where 'I can see clearly now', just as Jimmy Cliff said...

"I can see clearly now the rain has gone, I can see all obstacles in my way.

Gone are the dark clouds that had my blind. It's gonna be a bright, bright, sunshiny day."

For me it's now a sunshiny life.

I can trust myself, but the best feeling is that others trust me too, and that means more than anything.

A highlight for me, which I remember is picking the boys up from school. Feeling so proud to see those smiles it made me cry. Taking them on their first road trip out for lunch, it was priceless. The simple things mean the most in life.

I have my life back at long last and my mental health is in the background where it will stay.

Seeing my reflection return to the mirror I knew the fog had lifted and disappeared. That being said, I am now aware when things may trigger me and the risk is always there.

This is why I share and use my toolkit for my own health and well-being, and with the hope of helping others. With helping you.

I had to unlearn behaviour I witnessed growing up. I had to break a cycle.

As a mum, I could have done things differently. I'm not excusing things that have happened. But now I can see even more clearly where things went wrong. It wasn't fair for my daughter to take on the role of mum, while I was unable to fulfil this for her. It breaks my heart that she was forced to take this on, but I am so grateful for her love and support.

I feel so proud to be Mum again. I am determined to be the best Nanna I can for the boys. Breaking this cycle now, acknowledging the wrongs, the past and the triggers that pulled the carpet from under my feet. I hope this allows all who've been part of my journey to move forward with me.

"Sometimes your worst enemy is your own memory. Let it go."

I never thought I would have a breakdown. I thought I was strong. But sometimes we take on too much or have so much trauma to deal with, our body just shuts down to protect us.

On the road to recovery this is when you get to know how strong you really are. With the support and strength from others, family, friends and medical professionals you then can begin to start your climb of the mountain.

"Step into my shoes and live the life I've lived. And if you get as far as I have, just maybe you'll see how strong I really am."

This next chapter of life is so exciting, the future is bright.

Family and friends can be your strength. And above all self-belief and knowing that you are worthy is important. Also, you can do anything you put your mind to.

I live with heartache daily missing my pot of gold, but I find comfort in knowing his spirit is with me always. I see the smiles on the children's faces knowing they have Nanna back.

I am so grateful to you, the reader, for getting this far. I truly hope that this book, my words and the lived experiences that I've shared have given you some comfort with the parts you may resonate with. Most importantly I hope that it has helped you in knowing that you aren't alone and that there are things you can do to help yourself and help others understand – maybe pass them a copy of this book and ask them to read it.

Simply THANK YOU! But "thank you" doesn't seem enough.

Like Andrew Golds says in his song I want to...

"Thank you for being a friend.

Thank you for being a friend.

Thank you for being a friend.

Thank you for being a friend."

I've too many people to list but without all of your support and belief in me I couldn't win this battle and be the person I am today. I love you all xx

-   *Tina*

TINA'S TOOLS:

1   Be kind to yourself & show yourself love

2   Get dressed even if you don't feel like it

3   Take deep breaths & count to ten

4   Know your triggers

5   Take medication & consider alternative therapies

ABOUT THE AUTHOR

Tina Roberts started out her working life as a children's nanny in London which she loved. After a few years she returned home to Leicester where she worked in the hosiery and knitwear industry for a number of years.

Becoming a wife and then a mum, Tina considers this the first chapter in her adult life. On a journey of twists and turns a second marriage, and the second chapter, brought her on an adventure to Wales. Her third and final chapter is one which she is now living, include meeting her 'pot of gold' Harry.

Through childhood and adult life Tina has been faced with numerous traumatic experiences which have undoubtedly contributed to her illnesses and mental health.

'No Reflection' has been part of Tina's healing journey, which is still ongoing. Her aim is to make others aware that mental health is a part of everyday living for many people. Daily battles and struggles are apparent. It does not mean anyone impacted is "daft or stupid" or needing to be locked up. People need time and support to feel more stable and to get well.

Tina's message is that "Family and friends can be your strength. And above all self-belief and knowing that you are worthy is important. Also, you can do anything you put your mind to."

Through the book Tina shares her tools to help others as prompts, as these are what have helped her come to where she is now.

Attending art class has brought out her creative side, enjoying mindful moments while painting and drawing her favourite images. Being part of the choir literally makes her heart sing. Above all else having her family, her grandsons and her friends in her life makes her complete once again.

For Tina this book is the icing on the cake. She has been able to work through and share so much of her life and try to make sense of the experiences she has endured. It has allowed her a great deal of reflection time, where she can see her actions and reactions to situations and to life. This has allowed her to have more acceptance and become more at peace with things.

"I'm hoping my book helps all who are struggling, whether you are living with mental health issues or your family or friend is. I want to make people realise that mental health is all around us and normal people can be impacted. It doesn't matter what your profession is. Whether you're a doctor or a nurse yourself, or a firefighter or a teacher, anyone can be affected. Treat people as you wish to be treated." – Tina Wendy Roberts

NO REFLECTION

NO REFLECTION

NO REFLECTION

NO REFLECTION

NO REFLECTION

Printed in Great Britain
by Amazon